W9-CES-929

America's Leaders

The War on Terrorism

By Jill C. Wheeler

Visit us at
www.abdopub.com

Published by ABDO & Daughters, an imprint of ABDO Publishing Company, 4940 Viking Drive, Suite 622, Edina, Minnesota 55435.

Printed in the United States.

Edited by Paul Joseph
Graphic Design: John Hamilton
Cover Design: Mighty Media
Photos: AP/Wide World, DoD

Library of Congress Cataloging-in-Publication Data

Wheeler, Jill C., 1964-
    America's leaders / Jill C. Wheeler.
        p. cm. — (War on terrorism)
    Includes index.
    Summary: Discusses the leadership of George W. Bush, Dick Cheney, and
    many other powerful political and military players following the
    terrorist attacks of September 11, 2001.
    ISBN 1-57765-661-X
    1. United States—Politics and government—2001—Juvenile literature.
    2. September 11 Terrorist Attacks, 2001— Juvenile literature. 3. War
on Terrorism, 2001—Juvenile literature. 4. Political
leadership—United States—History—21st century—Juvenile literature.
5. Bush, George W. (George Walker), 1946—Juvenile literature. 6.
Cabinet officers—United States—History—21st century—Juvenile
literature. 7. Legislators—United States—History—21st
century—Juvenile literature.   [1. United States—Politics and
government—2001— 2. September 11 Terrorist Attacks, 2001. 3. War on
Terrorism, 2001— 4. Political leadership. 5. Bush, George W. (George
Walker), 1946— 6. Cabinet officers. 7. Legislators.]   I.Title. II. Series
    E902 .W48 2002
    973.931'092'2—dc21
                                                                                    2001056540

Table Of Contents

Terrorist Attack

Hijacked United Airlines Flight 175 slices through the South Tower of the World Trade Center.

The End Of Normal

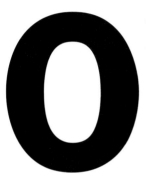

OON SEPTEMBER 11, 2001, PEOPLE WHO awoke early found few surprises in their morning newspapers. There was talk of more tax cuts to stimulate the sluggish economy. President Bush was visiting Florida and asking Congress to pass his education package. In the Middle East, Israeli and Palestinian officials were talking again of peace.

By mid-morning, Americans learned with sadness and rage that hijacked airplanes had slammed into and destroyed the two towers of New York's World Trade Center. A third hijacked airplane had cartwheeled into the Pentagon. A fourth crashed in what authorities believed was a failed suicide hijacking. In the span of a few hours, thousands of Americans were killed.

The prime suspect in the murders was Saudi millionaire Osama bin Laden and his al-Qaeda (al-KIGH-duh) terrorist network, supported by the Taliban government of Afghanistan.

With the Twin Towers reduced to rubble and thousands missing and presumed dead, Americans turned to their leaders. People found themselves discussing the actions of federal officials they had known little about before the attacks. And political leaders found themselves put to tests they never could have imagined before September 11, 2001.

Commander In Chief

President George W. Bush views the damaged Pentagon while flying in the Marine One helicopter.

Commander In Chief

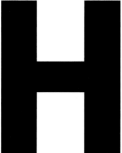

HISTORY HAS SHOWN THAT MOST HEROES are forged in times of crisis. Historic leaders such as United States President Franklin Delano Roosevelt and British Prime Minister Winston Churchill are remembered most for their heroism during World War II.

There was no world war on the horizon during the presidential election of November 2000. There was only a war of beliefs between Democrats and Republicans. When the polls closed, it became clear Americans were equally divided on how their nation should be governed. The vote was split almost evenly, and political analysts warned of trouble ahead. Such a split meant there was no clear mission for the new president. The person who finally captured the presidency would have to lead almost as many people who did not vote for him as who did. Whoever won would also have to deal with an equally divided Congress. The new president likely would face endless arguments for the next four years.

George W. Bush won the presidency by the narrowest margin in the history of the United States. He faced an especially tough task. Bush desperately needed to earn the respect of at least half of the American people. During his presidential campaign, critics mercilessly accused Bush of being inexperienced. He had served as governor of Texas, but that had been his only major political experience. The rest of his experience had been in the oil business and with professional sports teams.

If the newly elected president was discouraged about the challenges he faced, George W. Bush did not show it. "Whether you voted for me or not, I will do my best to serve your interests," he said in his acceptance speech in December 2000. "I will work to earn your respect." Despite his critics, President Bush believed he had a mission to serve the American people. He felt that even more strongly after September 11.

Americans saw very little of their president in the hours after the attacks. Bush was shuttled from one secure location to another in order to protect his safety. Later that afternoon, he demanded that he return to Washington. When the public saw him again, they saw a determined leader.

Before September 11, Bush had little experience with foreign policy. News reporters had seemed to enjoy quizzing him about international issues just to watch him search for an answer. Suddenly, with his nation at war, Bush immersed himself in world politics. He began reaching out to other leaders around the world. He asked for their help in the war on terrorism. Calmly, he requested the facts from his advisers. He listened, and he evaluated what to do next.

Touring the Devastation

President Bush views the damaged Pentagon. He later thanked rescue workers and volunteers for their efforts.

Early in the afternoon of September 11, President Bush gave a statement to the nation. He wrote the words himself. He never had been considered a great speaker, but this time he spoke from the heart. When he returned to Washington, D.C., he talked with his staff about what to say that evening. He rejected their idea of talking about "swift justice." He wanted to be honest with the American people. He wanted to warn them of the long struggle ahead.

Later that night, he gathered a group of advisers in a secure bunker deep underneath the White House. He wanted to make sure they knew the depth of his commitment to justice. Gathered with him were Vice President Dick Cheney, Secretary of State Colin Powell, National Security Adviser Condoleezza Rice, and Attorney General John Ashcroft. "Make no mistake," he told them. "Understand my resolve, and all of your people need to understand this."

Bush always had been patient and methodical when making decisions. Those close to him say he became even more so following the attacks. Almost every day he arrived at the Oval Office at daybreak and began reading the briefing books his staff had prepared. Then he prepared for a long day of meetings and phone calls. In the afternoon, he took a break to jog on a treadmill. Sometimes he jogged outside on the White House grounds. He said the exercise helped clear his head to make wise decisions.

Bush's work didn't stop on weekends. He continued his schedule of meetings with advisers. He became commander in chief of a war with two fronts. One front was in Afghanistan. The other front was at home. Bush had to calm a terrorized nation. "I ask you to live your lives, and hug your children," he said in an address to Congress on September 20. "I know many citizens have fears tonight, and I ask you to be calm and resolute...."

Bush also knew he had to follow his own advice. In a defiant gesture, the former managing partner of the Texas Rangers accepted an invitation to throw out the first pitch in the third game of the World Series. Standing on the pitcher's mound in Yankee Stadium, with no secret service agents to protect him, he wound up, threw, and delivered a strike. It sent a clear message to the world. Neither the U.S. nor its president would be bullied.

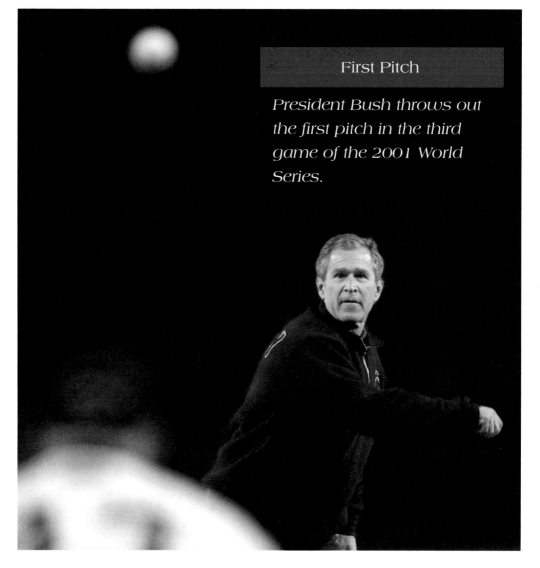

First Pitch

President Bush throws out the first pitch in the third game of the 2001 World Series.

Trusted Adviser

National Security Adviser Condoleezza Rice briefs reporters at the White House.

National Security

VEN BEFORE HIS ELECTION, BUSH HAD SAID he believed in delegating. He said the secret to effective government was to put together a team of skilled people and demand results from them. True to his word, he pulled together an incredible team. Political analysts called it the A-Team.

On the morning of September 11, President Bush was visiting an elementary school in Sarasota, Florida, when he learned of the attacks. Almost immediately, he got a call from a member of the A-Team. It was National Security Adviser Condoleezza Rice.

Rice is the only woman on Bush's A-Team and the first female national security adviser. She's used to pressure. As an African-American girl growing up in segregated Birmingham, Alabama, Rice said she'd had to be "twice as good" as everyone else.

A brilliant scholar, Rice started college at age 15 after skipping two grades. She had planned to major in music. Her mother also was a musician and had named her daughter after the musical term *con dolcezza*, which means "with sweetness." In college, Rice took a class on Russian politics. The teacher was Josef Korbel, father of former Secretary of State Madeleine Albright. Rice became fascinated by all things Russian and changed her course of studies.

National Security at Stake

Condoleezza Rice advises President Bush.

Rice stayed in the academic world for several years. At age 38, she became the second-highest official at Stanford University. In 1989, her Russian affairs expertise resulted in a job working for President George H.W. Bush as the National Security Council's director of Soviet and East European Affairs. During George W. Bush's campaign for president, Rice was his foreign policy adviser.

As national security adviser, Rice's role in the Bush administration increased dramatically after the September 11 attacks. In the months following, she barely left the president's side. Bush considers Rice a trusted friend, as well as a savvy adviser. She was influential in helping the president craft his foreign policy strategy.

Rice's Russian expertise was especially helpful. For years, the former Soviet Union had been dealing with problems in the Middle East, including terrorists. The Soviet Union even waged its own long and unsuccessful war in Afghanistan. Rice realized Russia's experience there could greatly help the U.S. in its war on terrorism—if Russia agreed to work with the United States. Part of Rice's job was to see that Russia did just that.

As national security adviser, Rice also had the job of briefing reporters on key policy issues. She told reporters how the administration was working to freeze the al-Qaeda network's financial assets. Al-Qaeda "will ultimately not be able to function if it cannot have access to money," she said. She even granted an interview to the Arab television network al-Jazeera.

Rice also restated the president's commitment to hunt down Osama bin Laden and his operatives. "The best defense is going to be a good offense," she said. "To go after these terrorists where they live."

Briefing the Public

Condoleezza Rice at a White House press conference.

Preparing Americans

After the terrorist attacks, Vice President Cheney said, "... We know with absolute certainty that... we will prevail."

Second In Command

VICE PRESIDENT DICK CHENEY WAS IN THE West Wing of the White House the morning of September 11 when secret service agents burst in. "We have to move, we're moving now, sir," they said as they rushed him off to a bunker on the White House grounds. From there Cheney directed the initial response to the attacks. From the bunker he spoke on the phone with President Bush every 30 minutes. He also spoke with other key officials. Cheney's immediate task was to find out as much as he could about what had happened so that he could advise the president. He told President Bush to head to a safe military base.

Cheney was no stranger to crises. The Nebraska native had worked in the government since 1969 and had served as chief of staff for President Gerald Ford in the mid-1970s. In 1989, he again answered a president's call to duty. This time, Cheney served as secretary of defense under President George H.W. Bush. In that position, he was instrumental in developing the U.S. strategy for the Persian Gulf War in 1991.

In the weeks following the September 11 attacks, Cheney worked quietly behind the scenes. He participated in national security meetings through a secure videoconference link. He also made calls to world leaders and members of Congress.

17

Due to security concerns, Cheney rarely appeared with President Bush. Under the U.S. Constitution, if the president is harmed or cannot carry out his duties, the vice president steps in. For that reason, the two officials must be kept in different locations if there is a threat to the president's safety.

Since the first day of the Bush administration, Cheney has been the president's top adviser. As a former congressman, Cheney has played a special role in the Bush administration's relations with Congress. To no one's surprise, even though Cheney could not be in the same location as the president, he spoke with Bush often.

Immediately following the attacks, officials often would not announce where Cheney was, just in case terrorists were looking for him. Cheney's aides often told him that people were wondering where he was. It even became a joke. "Don't tell them where I am," the vice president would answer with a grin.

As the days wore on, Cheney and the president rarely were seen together. Despite the distance, Cheney continued to advise President Bush, just as he had advised the president's father, George H.W. Bush. Cheney attended hundreds of meetings via telephone.

Cheney also took on the job of helping the American people cope with the new reality. He warned that there was now a war, and a war meant casualties. He also warned that the battle would not be swift. "Many of the steps we have now been forced to take will become permanent in American life," he said. "They represent an understanding of the world as it is, and dangers we must guard against perhaps for decades to come."

Second in Command

Vice President Cheney in the White House Oval Office after a briefing with President Bush.

Secretary of Defense

Secretary of Defense Donald Rumsfeld gives a press briefing at the Pentagon.

A War Like No Other

O N SEPTEMBER 12, 2001, PRESIDENT BUSH told Americans that the attacks on the World Trade Center and the Pentagon had been acts of war. Now, he said, the U.S. was going to fight a war against terrorism. It would take time, he cautioned. President Bush asked Americans to be patient.

Behind the scenes, Bush's military advisers understood all too well that this would be a different kind of war. The September 11 attacks had been compared to the Japanese attack on Pearl Harbor, which had pulled the U.S. into World War II. But there were several differences. In World War II, America knew who its enemies were, and where they were. In the war on terrorism, the enemies were not clearly defined, and most were hiding.

However, there was one similarity. It was likely that the war on terrorism would involve military action. That meant Secretary of Defense Donald Rumsfeld would be a key player.

The blunt-talking, no-nonsense Rumsfeld was ideal for the job. In 1975, he became the nation's youngest secretary of defense. A native of Illinois and a former naval aviator, Rumsfeld had a long and varied resume. He was elected to Congress at age 30, and then held jobs under Presidents Richard Nixon and Gerald Ford.

Rumsfeld became White House chief of staff under President Ford before taking the defense secretary position. In 1977, Rumsfeld took a break from politics and worked as a corporate executive helping struggling companies become profitable.

On September 11, Rumsfeld was in his third-floor office in the Pentagon. He was meeting with some members of Congress to discuss missile defenses. The issue was part of a larger project Rumsfeld had been working on. He wanted to overhaul the U.S. military. The military had been designed to fight the Cold War. He thought since the Cold War was over, it was time to retool. Rumsfeld wanted to turn the U.S. military into a high-tech, highly mobile fighting force. The new military would be better prepared to fight the more unconventional wars officials believed lay ahead.

One of those unconventional wars might include terrorism. Ironically, the talk in the meeting had turned to terrorism when Rumsfeld and the others felt the crash on the other side of the building. Immediately, Rumsfeld ran to the point of impact and began helping move injured people onto stretchers. He kept helping survivors until he was forced to stop. He spent much of the rest of the day on the phone with President Bush, Vice President Cheney, and others.

As the days wore on, Rumsfeld faced a new challenge. As the Pentagon's leader, he had to craft the U.S. military response to the attacks. He, along with Colin Powell, also had to brief key congressional leaders on the latest developments in the situation. They also attended daily National Security Council meetings with the president and vice president. On September 25, Rumsfeld announced that the anti-terrorism campaign would be called Operation Enduring Freedom. He also warned that it would not be like other wars.

"This is not something that begins with a significant event and ends with a significant event," he said. "The truth is, this is not about revenge. It's not about retaliation. This is about self-defense. The only way we can defend against terrorism is by taking the fight to the terrorists."

Before September 11, there had been rumors that Rumsfeld was on his way out of the Pentagon. The rumors quickly ended. "They've got the right guy at the right time, at the right job, and I think we're lucky as Americans," said former Senator Bob Dole. Added a reporter who profiled Rumsfeld, "People say he hates to lose, and he rarely does."

Thanking the Troops

Donald Rumsfeld is greeted by a pilot during a visit to a U.S. air base in Turkey.

Central Command

Four-star General Tommy Franks briefs reporters at a Pentagon news conference.

The Front Lines

ON OCTOBER 7, U.S. AND BRITISH FORCES began a military campaign aimed at eliminating international terrorism. The campaign had several objectives. One was to destroy the network of al-Qaeda terrorist bases in Afghanistan. Another objective was to bring Osama bin Laden to justice. Yet another objective was to topple Afghanistan's Taliban government. The extremist Taliban supported terrorist networks such as al-Qaeda.

The military campaign had three key leaders. They included Rumsfeld, Joint Chiefs of Staff Chairman Richard Myers, and four-star general Tommy Franks.

Franks was commander in chief of the U.S. Central Command (USCENTCOM), which is responsible for U.S. security interests from North Africa across the Arabian Peninsula to Central Asia. A 36-year Army veteran, he received three Purple Heart medals in the Vietnam War and served in the Persian Gulf War. As commander in chief, he oversees the U.S. Army, Navy, Air Force, and Marine units that operate in his region. He took charge of USCENTCOM just months before the terrorist attack on the USS *Cole* in October 2000.

Osama bin Laden is believed to have been behind the attack on the USS *Cole*, which took the lives of 17 American sailors. One year later, the quiet, determined Franks was charged with hunting down bin Laden. When asked how long the military was prepared to work toward that end, Franks merely replied, "As long as it takes." He enlisted the support of the Northern Alliance, the enemy of the Taliban, to help.

Assisting Franks were General Richard Myers and Lieutenant General Charles Wald. Myers had been vice chairman of the Joint Chiefs of Staff for more than a year. He was a fighter pilot in the Vietnam War and is a former commander of the U.S. Space Command. Wald was commander of USCENTCOM's air forces. He helped direct the air strikes in Bosnia in 1995. Under Operation Enduring Freedom, he oversaw the air strikes on Afghanistan.

While the military focused most of its attention overseas, the U.S. Marine Corps also created a new anti-terrorism force at home. The Anti-Terrorism Battalion of the Fourth Marine Expeditionary Brigade has the ability to move soldiers anywhere in the U.S. within six hours of a crisis. The brigade came under the command of Brigadier General Douglas O'Dell, a 33-year Marine veteran. He said the unit would be on guard to protect Americans from chemical and biological attacks.

Marines must undergo special training for the job, including experience in city environments. It is just one more reminder of how the war on terrorism will be different from anything else U.S. soldiers have ever known.

War Games

Members of the Marines' anti-terrorism unit role-play a terrorist attack.

On The Home Front

WORLD WAR II IS REMEMBERED AS A two-front war. America's war on terrorism is the same, but instead of Japan and Germany, the U.S. must fight terrorists abroad and at home. Just days after the attacks, President Bush created a new cabinet position called head of homeland security. The position would be in charge of coordinating U.S. efforts to defend against terrorism. Bush named Pennsylvania Governor Tom Ridge to head the office. He was sworn in to the new job on October 8, 2001.

Ridge had been a friend of Bush for a long time. Some people thought Bush would make him part of his cabinet. A former congressman and two-term governor of Pennsylvania, Ridge also fought in the Vietnam War. His actions there earned him the Bronze Star. As governor of Pennsylvania, he was known for being tough on crime. Now, the president was asking him to get tough with the security of Americans.

Ridge took on a staggering job. He had to coordinate with more than 40 different federal agencies, ranging from the Federal Bureau of Investigation (FBI) to the Department of Energy. Ridge and his staff had to consider how terrorists might harm

28

Americans. They had to consider every water supply, every food supply, and every transportation system a potential target.

In addition, days before Ridge took office, a Florida magazine employee died from anthrax. Then, less than a week into his job, Ridge learned that an intern in the mailroom of U.S. Senator Tom Daschle's office had been exposed to anthrax in a letter. So had people in the offices of NBC-TV in New York City.

As investigators and health officials scrambled to determine where the anthrax spores had come from, more anthrax exposures came to light. The spores were at CBS-TV offices, at the *New York Post* offices, and in several other buildings on Capitol Hill. Worst of all, in late October, two U.S. Postal Service workers died from anthrax. Investigators believed they had handled some of the tainted mail while en route to its destination.

Ridge worked hard to assess the public risk from the anthrax attacks. He became frustrated as he discovered there were more questions than answers. He asked for more scientists to help track down more clues. He met with President Bush to fill him in on the latest developments. And he struggled to make sure he was kept informed of new information gathered by the FBI, the CIA, and the other agencies he was charged with coordinating.

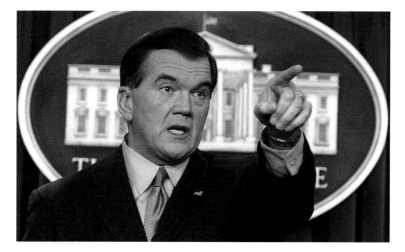

Homeland Security Director Tom Ridge answers questions at a White House press briefing.

New Laws, New Scares

THE EVENING AFTER THE ATTACKS, SPEAKER of the House Republican J. Dennis Hastert and House Democratic Leader Dick Gephardt vowed that both political parties would "stand shoulder to shoulder to fight this evil." Suddenly, it seemed as though both political parties had put aside their differences over the 2000 election. They had a new common enemy, and it was time to fight back.

It wasn't the first time Hastert, of Illinois, and Gephardt, of Missouri, had showed their unity. As Speaker, Hastert is the government's third-ranking elected official. When he took the position in January 1999, he broke tradition to briefly share leadership of the House with Gephardt. A former wrestling coach, Hastert believes in the power of teamwork. Likewise, Gephardt has said he believes good legislation comes from cooperation.

Congress needed that cooperation, and fast. Several major laws needed to be passed. President Bush received congressional approval on an anti-terrorism bill. The bill passed by both houses on October 26, granting federal authorities more tools to watch suspected terrorists and gather information.

In the midst of the conflict, the anthrax-laced letter arrived at the office of Senate Majority Leader Tom Daschle. Investigators quickly tried to determine how far the anthrax had spread and if other congressional offices had received tainted letters. Rumors about anthrax contamination swirled around Capitol Hill. Thousands of workers lined up to be tested for anthrax exposure. Congressional leaders struggled with what to do in the face of so many questions.

On October 17, Hastert, Gephardt, Daschle, and Senate Minority Leader Trent Lott met with President Bush. They discussed how to keep party politics from bogging down important legislation, such as the airport security measure. They also discussed how far the anthrax had spread around Capitol Hill.

Following the meeting, Gephardt and Hastert decided to adjourn the House. Already, some House and Senate offices were closed for contamination sweeps. Some members of Congress were returning home to reassure anxious constituents. Others were operating out of makeshift offices in other buildings. Some even set up offices using card tables and cell phones in Capitol Hill parking lots.

Daschle and Lott agreed to keep the Senate in session throughout the ordeal. A native of South Dakota, Daschle has remained close to his hardworking farm roots. Each year, he travels across the state alone in a rental car with no staff members and no agenda. Daschle says the annual visit helps him keep things in perspective. It also reminds him how much people are counting on him and the rest of Congress.

Lott grew up in Mississippi, the son of a sharecropper turned shipyard worker. He has represented his state since 1972 and continues to earn Mississippians' respect—and his re-election. Despite the anthrax attacks, the two men were determined to do business.

Another part of Congress' business dealt with the economy. With a recession looming, senators and representatives went to work on an economic stimulus package. They hoped to prevent the September 11 attacks from damaging more American businesses.

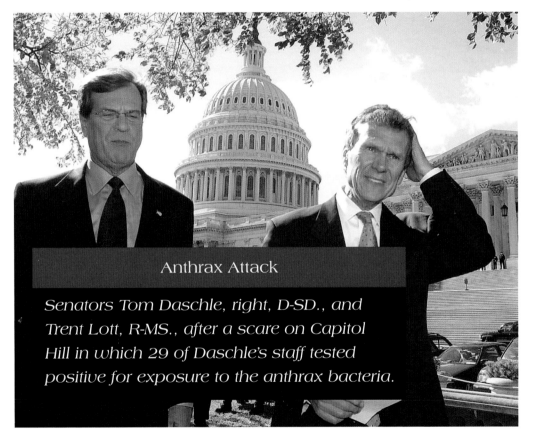

Anthrax Attack

Senators Tom Daschle, right, D-SD., and Trent Lott, R-MS., after a scare on Capitol Hill in which 29 of Daschle's staff tested positive for exposure to the anthrax bacteria.

Quiet Diplomacy

Secretary of State Colin Powell works to make sure American allies join the war against terrorism.

Delicate Negotiations

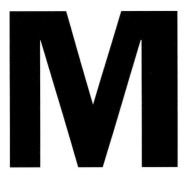

MOST ANALYSTS AGREE THAT THE U.S. cannot win the war on terrorism alone. President Bush will need the support and cooperation of other nations. He has been busy getting that support. So has his secretary of state, retired four-star General Colin Powell.

The son of Jamaican immigrants, Powell became the first African American to hold the military's highest office, chairman of the Joint Chiefs of Staff. He served two tours of duty in the Vietnam War and played a key role in planning and executing the Persian Gulf War. Some people hoped Powell would run for president. When Bush asked Powell to serve on his cabinet, Powell readily agreed.

On the morning of September 11, Powell was having breakfast with the president of Peru when one of his aides handed him a note. It said that an airplane had struck the World Trade Center. Later, when Powell learned the crash was not an accident, he cut short his trip to Latin America and returned to Washington, D.C. He then began working quietly behind the scenes.

Analysts said Powell was unique in the Bush administration. While many of his fellow cabinet members thought the U.S. should mind its own business, Powell believed the U.S. was part of a global community. A political moderate, he believed the U.S. government needed to adopt a worldview.

Immediately following the attacks, Powell contacted leaders in more than 80 nations around the world. He sought and gained support from many of them on a variety of fronts. Some agreed to let the U.S. use their air space or military bases for military actions. Others offered to help with intelligence or arrest terrorists. Still others pledged military support. As the war on terrorism waged on, Powell turned his focus to holding that coalition of nations together under increasing international concerns. Like Condoleezza Rice, he did an interview with the Arab television network al-Jazeera.

Always cool under fire, Powell understood the fine line the U.S. was walking in the new war. He wanted to be sure the attack on Afghanistan was not viewed as an attack against Arabs or the religion of Islam. Powell fought to limit the attacks to the al-Qaeda organization. Others in the Bush administration wanted to attack other terrorist-harboring nations, such as Iraq. Powell disagreed. The Vietnam War taught him that it would be a mistake to go into a war with no clear objectives.

Powell and Secretary of Defense Donald Rumsfeld met regularly with congressional leaders to brief them on events. Powell, Rice, Cheney, and Rumsfeld gathered with the president nightly to review the day's events and plan for the next. Somehow, they had to stay ahead of the terrorists and keep Americans behind the war effort.

Strategy Session

Colin Powell and Secretary of Defense Donald Rumsfeld meet at the White House.

Team Players

Attorney General John Ashcroft looks on as FBI Director Robert Mueller discusses the anthrax threat.

Tracking The Terrorists

THE FEDERAL INVESTIGATION INTO THE September 11 attacks became the largest criminal investigation in American history. It began just minutes after the attacks occurred. By Tuesday afternoon, the National Security Agency had the first lead. They had intercepted two messages. They believed the messages showed that terrorists linked to Osama bin Laden had carried out the attacks. By Wednesday morning, federal officials said they knew the terrorists had held pilot's licenses. They had leads linking them to terrorist cells in Massachusetts, Florida, and Canada.

The investigation progressed under the leadership of two men. U.S. Attorney General John Ashcroft heads the U.S. Department of Justice. Robert Mueller is the director of the FBI. September 11 was only Mueller's seventh day on the job.

Even before the attacks, Mueller knew he had a tough job ahead. The FBI had been badly battered in recent years. They had discovered one of their agents had been spying for Russia, and they had failed to turn over important documents in the Oklahoma City bombing case.

Ashcroft was one of the people who asked President Bush to put Mueller in charge of the FBI. Mueller had served as Ashcroft's acting deputy attorney general. A decorated Vietnam War vet, Mueller began his career at a private law firm in San Francisco. He became an assistant U.S. attorney in San Francisco, and worked his way up the public ranks. Between 1990 and 1993, he worked for President George H.W. Bush as the head of the Justice Department's Criminal Division. Before taking the deputy attorney general job, he worked in the homicide section of the U.S. Attorney's Office for the District of Columbia.

Officials within the FBI and Justice Department have not always worked well together. Many past administrations have seen their share of turf wars. Sometimes the FBI director and the attorney general were actually hostile to one another. Mueller and Ashcroft ended that pattern. The two worked together virtually non-stop throughout the investigation.

Mueller set up a special office for Ashcroft in the FBI's operations center in Washington, D.C. The center was created following the 1993 World Trade Center bombing. Its mission is to make it easier for state and local law enforcement agencies to share important information with the FBI.

Ashcroft arrived at the center almost every morning at 7:30 A.M. There, he was surrounded by hundreds of FBI agents who worked alongside officials of the Justice Department and the Central Intelligence Agency (CIA). He gave several interviews each day and quickly became the voice of the investigation.

No other attorney general in recent years has been so deeply involved in an investigation. The attorney general is the chief law officer of the government. He or she must begin and oversee those legal proceedings that affect the welfare of the American people. It is a very important job and often a controversial one.

Ashcroft himself was a controversial candidate for the job. A lawyer by training, he served two terms as governor of Missouri and represented Missouri in the Senate. Ashcroft is known for his conservative views. He is in favor of the death penalty and is opposed to gun control. Some critics have claimed that he is a racist because he opposed desegregating schools in his home state of Missouri. His supporters say Ashcroft is a man of deep conviction and strong principles.

That conviction became useful as Ashcroft tackled the huge September 11 attack investigation. One of his colleagues said the investigation became a very personal mission for the attorney general. Likewise, it had become the mission of the FBI.

The FBI was formed to fight crime—things like illegal drug sales, car theft, and organized crime. After the attacks, FBI agents were asked to fight a secret network of terrorist cells. Agents quickly began working with state and local law enforcement officials to find clues. They also had to gather information that might prevent future attacks.

Ashcroft and Mueller issued a public warning on October 11. They said there was a possibility of more terrorist attacks. They encouraged Americans to go about their business as usual. But they urged them to be on the lookout for anything suspicious.

By late October, the FBI had received more than 400,000 leads and tips related to the hijackings. There were just over 11,000 FBI agents to follow up on all those leads. In addition, there were the anthrax letters to investigate. Mueller quickly began holding meetings every dawn with key FBI officials. They would review the latest information so they could brief Ashcroft and President Bush.

The President was demanding answers. Ashcroft, Mueller, and their respective agencies were determined to provide them.

Leader of New York

Mayor Rudy Giuliani rallied his stricken city after the terrorist attacks on the World Trade Center.

Heroes At Home

NEW YORK CITY MAYOR RUDY GIULIANI rushed to the World Trade Center as soon as he heard about the first crash. He was standing beneath the 110-story Twin Towers when the second plane struck. He also was one of the last people to see three top New York City Fire Department officials alive. Just minutes after he met with them, the firefighters were crushed by debris from the falling towers. Giuliani himself was showered with smoke and ash as the first tower collapsed.

In the terrifying first hours after the attacks, Mayor Giuliani became a spokesperson not just for a city, but for a nation. As President Bush was shuttled between secure locations, Giuliani talked with reporters and gave orders. He reassured the world that New York would survive the attacks.

Giuliani always had been a leader. He grew up in a working-class family in Brooklyn, New York. In school, he was voted "Class Politician" even though he never held elected office. As a grandson of Italian immigrants, he was raised with a fierce hatred of organized crime, called the Mafia. He channeled those feelings into a career as an attorney.

Giuliani eventually held the number three position in the U.S. Justice Department. Before running for mayor of New York City, he was U.S. attorney for the Southern District of New York. A brilliant cross-examiner, he gained a reputation as a tough prosecutor. He relentlessly went after white-collar criminals and mobsters alike.

That reputation helped Giuliani become the first Republican mayor of New York City in 20 years. During the campaign, he promised to reduce crime and improve the city's quality of life. During his two terms, he did just that. Yet it came with a price. Critics said he used the city police department like an army to achieve his objectives. Members of minority communities said he was insensitive to their concerns. Still, crime in the city fell by 30 percent and more tourists came to visit. Giuliani also reduced the city's welfare rolls by more than 100,000 people. That made him seem heartless to some people.

In the aftermath of September 11, even his critics had to agree Giuliani appeared warm and compassionate. He provided hourly updates to anxious family members and friends of people who were missing. He attended funerals and charity events. He rallied rescue workers at Ground Zero. He called for calm and asked people to avoid blaming any one group of people for the tragedy.

Always the politician, Giuliani made sure the right government officials toured the site. He especially liked to show them Ground Zero from a helicopter. "When you see it from the air, you realize how devastating it is," he said. "It just makes you angry, and it makes you determined."

Likewise, New York Governor George Pataki stepped up his efforts after the attacks. Elected to a second term in 1998, he was the state's first Republican chief executive. He was born on his family's farm in Peekskill, New York, and attended Yale and

Columbia Law School on academic scholarships. Before becoming governor, Pataki served in the state legislature for 10 years. He also served as mayor of his hometown.

Following the attacks, Pataki worked with state lawmakers to craft special anti-terrorism legislation. The legislation made it easier for law enforcement officers to catch terrorists. It also created stronger punishments for terrorist acts. He also announced plans to help family members of attack victims get a college education. He attended memorial ceremonies for fallen firefighters and other victims. In November, he announced plans for a special program that would work to rebuild the part of Manhattan devastated by the World Trade Center attacks.

New Yorkers were pleased with the moves. In June, polls showed Pataki's approval ratings at less than 60 percent. Following the attacks, they soared to more than 80 percent.

Likewise, Giuliani's popularity skyrocketed. England's Queen Elizabeth II honored Giuliani with an honorary knighthood for his help and support to British people who lost friends and loved ones in the tragedy. He even became the first U.S. mayor in 50 years to address the United Nations (U.N.) General Assembly. "This massive attack was intended to break our spirit," he told the U.N. delegates. "It has not done that. It has made us stronger, more determined, and more resolved."

Mexican President Vicente Fox, left, and New York Governor George Pataki, right, look on as New York City Mayor Rudolph Giuliani speaks to reporters after touring the destruction at the World Trade Center site.

Glossary

anthrax
A bacteria that causes an often fatal disease in humans and animals.

bunker
A sturdy room, usually underground, that can withstand an attack.

coalition
A group of organizations or countries that agree to work together.

Cold War
The struggle between the United States and its allies and the Soviet Union and its allies after World War II.

Northern Alliance
The organization of rebel Afghan soldiers fighting the Taliban.

Persian Gulf War
The 1990-91 conflict in which a U.S.-led coalition of soldiers forced Iraqi soldiers out of Kuwait.

Taliban
The ruling party of Afghanistan from 1996 to 2001.

terrorist cell
A small group of terrorists who work together.

Where On The Web?

http://www.whitehouse.gov/
The official web site of the White House. Information on President George W. Bush, Vice President Dick Cheney, and the rest of the president's cabinet.

http://www.defenselink.mil/osd/topleaders.html
Information on Secretary of Defense Donald Rumsfeld and the Defense Department.

http://www.state.gov/
Information on the United States State Department, including biographical information on Secretary of State Colin Powell.

http://www.usdoj.gov/
Information on the Department of Justice, and U.S. Attorney General John Ashcroft.

http://www.whitehouse.gov/homeland/
Information about the Office of Homeland Security and its director, Tom Ridge.

Index